SUCCESSFUL INDOOR GARDENING

EXOTIC
FLOWERING
HOUSEPLANTS

SUCCESSFUL INDOOR GARDENING
EXOTIC
FLOWERING
HOUSEPLANTS

William Davidson

HPBooks
a division of
PRICE STERN SLOAN
Los Angeles

A Salamander Book

Published by HP Books, a division of Price Stern Sloan, Inc.,
360 North La Cienega Boulevard, Los Angeles, California 90048.
Printed in Belgium.

9 8 7 6 5 4 3 2 1

Library of Congress Cataloging-in-Publication Data

Davidson, William.
　　Exotic flowering houseplants.

　　(Successful indoor gardening)
　　Includes index.
　　1. House plants.　2. Flowers.　I. Title.　II. Series.
SB419.D3673 1989　　　635.9′65　　89-2016
ISBN 0-89586-831-8

Credits

Introduction written by: David Squire
Editor: Geoffrey Rogers
Assistant editor: Lisa Dyer
Designer: Nigel Duffield
Photographer: Eric Crichton
Line artwork: Tyler/Camoccio Design Consultants
Filmset by: The Old Mill, London
Color separation by: Kentscan Ltd.
Printed by: Proost International Book Production, Turnhout, Belgium

Contents

Introduction

Flowering houseplants bring a wide range of colours to a home, some vibrant and bright, others subtle and demure, but all interesting and exciting. This informative guide will show you how to grow over 75 of the most sumptuous and exotic varieties of indoor flowering plants with complete success. To help you choose which type to buy, the species are grouped according to the ease with which they can be cultivated, and detailed growing instructions include such essential information as the light, water and temperature requirements of each plant.

Many flowering houseplants do not need high temperatures, even in winter, while others are more tropical in nature and require both warmth and high humidity. Flaming Katy *(Kalanchoe blossfeldiana)* and cyclamen both grow best in relatively cool conditions, while peace lilies *(Spathiphyllum)* need both high temperatures and humidity. There are, therefore, plants for every room of the house as well as every time of the year, and you don't have to have excessively warm conditions to create a blaze of colour.

Buying flowering houseplants
Choose your plants with care: some may live for many years and become part of the home. If poor specimens are bought, they seldom develop into strong and healthy plants so, to ensure success, follow these simple guidelines when buying flowering houseplants.
□ Always buy plants from reputable sources.
□ Don't buy plants which are displayed outside shops, especially in winter. Flowering plants which receive a cold shock may shed their buds at a later date, while in summer the compost soon becomes dry and causes wilting.
□ Ensure that there are plenty of unopened flower buds. If the flowers are fully open when a plant is bought, its display is limited. This is important when buying plants such as flaming

Above: Autumn-flowering plants, such as cyclamen, poinsettias and azaleas, create a blaze of colour that can last until Christmas.

Right: Always buy plants bearing plenty of flower buds. Those bought when the flowers are fully open will be short-lived.

Katy *(Kalanchoe blossfeldiana)* and the Persian violet *(Exacum affine)* which are discarded when their display is over.

- ☐ Don't buy plants infested with pests or diseases. Not only will the plants be marred, but they will infect others.
- ☐ Avoid plants with congested roots or those which have only recently been repotted.
- ☐ Don't buy plants with roots growing out of drainage holes. Also, avoid plants with algae or slime on the compost or pot.
- ☐ Avoid plants with dry or excessively wet compost.

Getting flowering plants home

Equally as important as selecting and buying the right plant is getting your plant home safely afterwards. Here are a few clues to success.

- ☐ Make buying flowering houseplants the last job on your shopping list: there is then less chance of the plant being damaged.
- ☐ Avoid putting plants in extremely cold car boots (trunks) in winter, or in very hot boots in summer. Instead, stand them in boxes placed inside the car, but safe from the ravages of young children or dogs.
- ☐ Ask for the plant to be wrapped in a plastic or paper sleeve, especially in winter when cold winds soon cause damage.
- ☐ Get your plant home as soon as possible, especially in winter.

Acclimatizing your new plants

Once you have got your plant home you should quickly establish it indoors as follows:

- ☐ Remove the wrapping from the plant as soon as you get home.
- ☐ Immediately place the plant in its permanent position, in good light. Avoid excessively strong and direct sunlight or cold draughts.
- ☐ Ensure that the compost is moist. If flowering plants wilt badly, the flowers as well as the newly-opening buds may be irreparably damaged.
- ☐ Avoid knocking flowering plants as this may cause the buds to fall off.

Getting the Best from Flowering Houseplants

The pleasure you get from a flowering houseplant — and the time it remains attractive — depends on the way you care for it. Flowering plants react more rapidly than foliage types to neglect, the flowers soon suffering. Here are a few ways to help you get the best from your plant.

Watering Keep the compost moist at all times when the plant is bearing flowers, but not so saturated with water that all air is excluded. Those plants which are retained from year to year will need a resting period after they have finished flowering or during winter, when little or no water is needed.

Some plants, such as azaleas, dislike lime both in their compost and in the water you give them. If your water is hard and limy, use water which has been boiled and allowed to cool. Alternatively, provided the water is only slightly alkaline, run the water for several minutes before collecting it in a watering-can, and then allow it to stand and settle before use. Most plants, however, live quite happily for years on tap water.

Feeding When a plant is potted, the compost has enough food in it to last six to eight weeks. Therefore, it is likely that by the time a plant is bought it needs to be fed. During the time it is in flower, give a weak liquid feed every two to three weeks. Many flowering plants are discarded when the flowers fade, but those which are retained for a further season need to be fed regularly until they reach their dormant stage, which is usually during the winter.

Mist spraying Plants from tropical and sub-tropical regions especially need a relatively humid atmosphere. Indeed, plants in general benefit from high humidity and a moderate temperature rather than low humidity and a high temperature. However, high humidity can encourage soft petals to be infected by disease.

The level of humidity can be increased by using a fine mist sprayer to lightly cover the surface of leaves with water droplets, but avoid any water falling on flowers. In winter, mist spray plants in the morning, so that the leaf surfaces are dry by nightfall. If water droplets remain on a leaf — and especially a flower — when the temperature falls at night, this encourages disease.

Temperature The temperature in which a houseplant is grown plays an important role in both its long- and short-term health. A plant grown in the home invariably has to fit in with the general temperature in a particular room — rather than the room being heated to a temperature which suits a specific plant — so, to help you decide where best to put a plant, we have indicated the ideal temperature range for each species.

Because centrally-heated homes usually have the heating turned down at night, it is probable that the temperature in even the warmest room will fall to below the recommended level for your plant. If this happens, keep the compost slightly drier than normal and ensure that the plant is not in a draught. And select only those plants which can be safely grown within the temperature range possible in your home.

Grooming This is an important daily task if plants are to look their best. Remove flowers as soon as they fade: if left, the dead flowers mar the plant and encourage others to decay. Also, by removing faded flowers, newly-developing buds are encouraged to open. Pull off the complete flower stalks of dead cyclamen flowers and plants that bear a mass of small flowers where the stalks join the stem. Small stalks which are left tend to encourage the entry of diseases, as well as spoiling the plant's appearance. Remove dead leaves from plants and wipe healthy leaves clean if dirty.

Compost Flowering plants which are bought when the buds are showing colour and subsequently discarded when flowering has finished do not need to be repotted. However, plants which are kept for several seasons may need to be repotted when their roots fill the pot. If the plant is growing in a loam-based compost repot it into a similar compost with a higher fertilizer content. Plants growing in a peat-based compost should be repotted into the same compost each time. Do not change from a loam-based type to a peat type, or *vice versa.*

Above: The roots of plants such as cyclamen can be kept cool by standing the pot on a layer of moist pebbles. This also helps to create a humid atmosphere around the leaves.

Displaying Flowering Houseplants

A flowering houseplant is always attractive, but if cleverly displayed to form a feature in a room — on its own or with other plants — its effect can be made even more eye-catching.

Table-top displays Dining room tables as well as coffee tables are popular places for plants. Round or oval tables demand symmetrical plants such as cinerarias, calceolarias and Persian violets. Give these plants a quarter turn every few days to prevent them growing towards the light and becoming lop-sided.

Group displays A display formed of three small flowering plants such as African violets always looks more impressive than a single plant. Leave the plants in their individual pots and stand them in a larger but shallow outer container. A grouping such as this looks good when on a large, oval or round polished table. Alternatively, an irregular-shaped group, with a flowering plant assuming a dominant position and surrounded by small flowering or foliage plants, creates an attractive feature in a corner or by the side of a patio window. These groups look well positioned on a low table.

Indoor hanging baskets These are similar to outdoor hanging baskets but have built into them a drip tray or the space for a plastic saucer in which to stand the flower pot. Both trailing and cascading flowering and foliage plants can be used. Flowering ones to look for include the Italian bellflower *(Campanula isophylla)*, trailing begonias, lipstick vine *(Aeschynanthus lobbianus)* and the goldfish plants *(Columnea* x *banksii* and *C. microphylla).*

Displays in troughs Plants can be displayed in small troughs, with the plants set to form either a pyramidal, rectangular or triangular outline. The triangular outline looks best when positioned with the tallest side in a corner of a room, whereas the others are best when displayed along a wall or near a window.

Illuminating plants Most plants benefit from being highlighted by a spotlight, especially in winter. However, the quality of light emitted by a tungsten-filament bulb is not the type that encourages plants to grow. Also, if placed too close, the heat generated by the bulb may burn the plant. Nevertheless, used in combination with dimmed room lights, spotlights can create an eye-catching effect.

The use of mirrors You can help turn your plant into the focal point of a room by placing it in front of a mirror. For this purpose, small mirrors are just as effective as large ones. If a space is left in a bookcase and a small mirror fitted into the area, with a plant positioned in front of it, this invariably forms an attractive feature.

Left: A display of houseplants looks good in an unused fire-place, but only place flowering plants there for a few days.

Above: Flowering houseplants make an attractive feature in a room when displayed in an imaginative range of containers.

Displays in fireplaces and alcoves In summer, the surrounds of fireplaces offer cool places for plants, especially shade-loving types. Flowering houseplants, however, need the best light they can get and usually these places are not well lit with natural light. Therefore, only put flowering plants there as a temporary display.

Natural recesses, especially between waist- and eye-height, are ideal for displaying flowering plants. If there is a convenient ledge on which a plant can be stood, either trailing or upright plants can be used. If, however, there is no ledge, fix a pot-supporting wall-bracket to the wall and use a trailing flowering plant — any of those suitable for an indoor hanging-basket are suitable.

Cache pots These attractive outer pots are ideal for enhancing clay or plastic pots lacking eye-appeal. They are usually ornate and attractively coloured plastic, but they can be pottery or ornate metal such as copper. Choose them to harmonize with the flower colours, not to dominate the display. Take care when using them that, through excessive watering, they do not contain stagnant water, which in winter keeps the compost too wet and encourages the onset of diseases.

Plants as camouflage Few homes are without a feature which is in need of camouflage, whether it is central-heating pipes, surfaced-laid electricity wires or water pipes. Plants can be used either to hide the unsightly feature or to draw attention away from it. A climbing plant strategically positioned provides the perfect camouflage. *Hoya carnosa* and *Stephanotis floribunda* are both challenging climbers, but always ensure that the foliage does not touch heating or hot-water pipes.

Good Health Guide

There are three main problems from which flowering houseplants are likely to suffer: pests which eat or suck flowers, leaves, stems and roots; diseases which can soon create an unsightly mess; and physiological disorders.

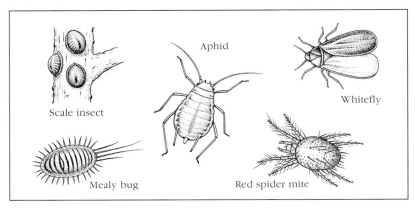

Aphid

Whitefly

Scale insect

Mealy bug

Red spider mite

Above: These are some of the pests that may attack your plants. To eradicate them, spray infested plants with pesticide.

Below: Don't let an infestation of aphids build up to this extent. Spray with pesticide immediately aphids appear.

Plant infesting pests

- **Aphids,** often known as greenfly, are plumpish green insects, with or without wings. They cluster around soft shoot tips and in flower buds, as well as in leaf joints. They suck the sap, weaken the plant and emit a sticky honeydew. To kill off these pests, spray infested plants with the appropriate pesticide.
- **Whitefly** are tiny, rather triangular-shaped white flies which cluster mainly on the undersides of soft leaves. Their larvae, which also live mainly on the undersides of leaves, deposit a sticky honeydew. To kill off these pests, spray infested plants with the appropriate pesticide.
- **Red spider mites** are minute, red, brownish-red or straw-coloured 'spiders' which infest houseplants, especially when the air is dry and the temperature high. Leaves assume yellow mottling and webbing may occur. Mist-spraying plants — but not the flowers — helps to control this pernicious pest. To kill them off, spray infested plants with the appropriate pesticide.
- **Mealy bugs** are slow-moving — eventually static — pests which resemble small and woolly woodlice. They usually cluster beneath leaves and in leaf joints. Light infestations can be controlled by using a moist cotton bud to wipe away the young bugs. Spray severely infested plants with pesticide.
- **Scale insects** are hard, brownish, static discs which cluster on the undersides of leaves and along stems. They are unsightly and severe infestations cause yellowing. They also create honeydew. Light infestations can be controlled with moist cotton buds, but established colonies are difficult to eradicate. Spray severely infested plants with the appropriate pesticide.

Plant diseases

- **Botrytis,** also known as grey mould, forms a grey, fluffy mould which can cover all the plant, but especially on flowers and soft leaves. Begonias, African violets and cyclamen are especially susceptible. Badly ventilated, still and cool conditions encourage its presence. Spray infected plants with fungicide and cut away badly infected parts. Destroy plants that are totally infected.
- **Sooty mould** is a black fungus which grows on the sticky excretion of aphids, whiteflies, scale insects and mealy bugs. Leaves become covered with a black, powdery deposit. Wipe the mould off with a damp cloth, then rinse the plant with clean water. Spray with fungicide to control sucking pests.
- **Powdery mildew** creates a disfiguring white, powdery coating or white fluffy growth on leaves. It may eventually attack flowers and stems. Remove and burn severely infected leaves and spray the rest of the plant with a fungicide.

Physiological disorders

These occur because a plant has not been given the correct treatment. Here are a few of the problems which can arise.
- **Wilting** happens mainly when the compost is kept too dry, but water-saturated compost also causes wilting. If the compost is dry, add water: if too wet, remove the soil-ball and allow it to partly dry before returning it to its pot.
- **Flower buds dropping off** or failing to open can occur if the plant is badly knocked, placed in a cold draught, given a cold position or if the compost is kept too dry or too wet.
- **Sun scald,** in the form of brown, papery patches, occurs on leaves and flowers which have been misted and then positioned in strong sunlight.

Easy to Grow

The range of flowering houseplants is wide, and although some species are difficult to grow and demand great care there are others which are easily grown and ideal for beginners. Many of these easy-to-grow plants are bought when they are beginning to produce flowers and discarded afterwards. They include cinerarias, the Persian violet (*Exacum affine*), *Celosia argentea* and flaming Katy (*Kalanchoe blossfeldiana*). A few are tuberous or bulbous and draw on their reserves of food and stored energy to create a spectacular display; the amaryllis and the zephyr flower (*Zephyranthes candida*) are examples. Some of these easy-to-grow plants, such as the Italian bellflower (*Campanula isophylla*), are relatively hardy and do not require high temperatures.

Aechmea fasciata
EXOTIC BRUSH
SILVER VASE
URN PLANT
VASE PLANT

The silvery-grey leaves have a light grey down on them that adds much to the attraction of this most excellent of all bromeliads. The grey leaves are broad and recurving and form a central chamber or urn, which should be filled with water. There are spines along the leaf margins, so be careful when handling. Also avoid touching the grey down on the leaves if the plants are to be seen to their best effect.

Young plants can be raised from seed, in which case bracts take some five to seven years to appear, or from basal shoots of mature plants, in which case bracts develop in two to three years.

The bract is a delightful soft pink in colour and, as if this were not enough, small but intensely blue flowers will also develop in the spiky pink bract. This is a truly fine plant that is easy to manage and will remain in 'flower' for up to nine months.

To encourage bloom:
Provide bright light and humid surroundings.

□ Good light
□ Temp: 13-18°C (55-65°F)
□ Keep urn filled with water

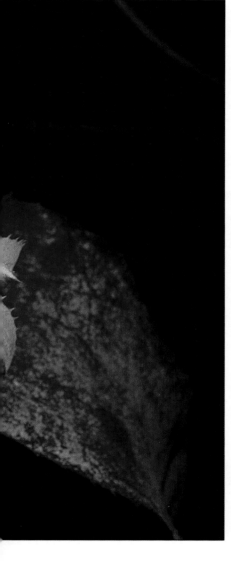

Left: Perhaps the most popular bromeliad, Aechmea fasciata has silver-banded green leaves and a beautiful tufted pink inflorescence. It will bloom readily and the colour lasts for months.

Begonia boweri
EYELASH BEGONIA
MINIATURE BEGONIA

There are a number of evergreen, fibrous-rooted begonias worth finding space for in the home, and this is one of the best of the more compact types. Flowers are white to pale pink in colour and though small in size, plentiful in number. The principal attraction, however, is the foliage, which is a mottled pale green and almost black in colour.

Growth is low and spreading, and the rhizomatous stem becomes gnarled in time, which tends to make plants less attractive as they shed their lower leaves. Rather than continue with an older and less attractive plant it is better to start fresh plants from sections of stem with a few leaves attached, or from individual leaves. Place leaves in shallow pans of fresh, moist peat at a temperature of not less than 18°C (65°F), and preferably in a closed propagator. Use peaty soil when potting on, and the plants will need moderate feeding and watering.

To encourage bloom:
Allow to grow potbound.

☐ Filtered light
☐ Temp: 13-18°C (55-65°F)
☐ Keep moist

Below: Begonia boweri is a delightful plant which has attractive mottled foliage and delicate flowers. This plant will thrive in moist surroundings.

Right: The golden-green leaves and orange-pink flower bracts of Billbergia pyramidalis make this easy-to-grow bromeliad a favourite plant for the home.

Billbergia pyramidalis
FOOLPROOF PLANT

Belonging to the bromeliad family, billbergias are very tolerant houseplants that will thrive more on neglect than on constant, fussing care. This species has golden green leaves and produces attractive spikes of orange-pink bracts and red and blue flowers at almost any time of the year. Individual bracts last for only a week or so, but each mature plant bears several spikes.

Grow this bromeliad in loose-textured, lime-free potting mix and water only when the top layer of soil has dried out. Use soft water or rain water if possible. Normal room temperatures and bright light will keep this plant perfectly healthy.

Billbergias are generally free of pests and diseases. Propagation is also no problem; simply remove and pot up the offsets that develop around the base of the parent plant.

To encourage bloom:
Keep in bright light.

□ Good light
□ Temp: 13-18°C (55-65°F)
□ Keep on the dry side

Calceolaria hybrids
POCKETBOOK PLANT
POUCH FLOWER
SLIPPER FLOWER
SLIPPERWORT

These pouch-like flowers are available in a bewildering range of colours. Many different strains are available and all will give a splendid display if a few standard rules are followed. First and foremost is that these plants must have good light, a loam-based mixture in which to grow, and regular feeding once they have filled their pots with roots.

When buying a mature plant from a retailer it is important to check the roots in the pot on getting the plant home; an overcrowded root system means the plant should be potted on straight away. It is also wise to give plants a general inspection before buying, particularly on the undersides of leaves, and to reject any that have pests present.

These are temporary plants and should be discarded after flowering.

Above: Calceolaria hybrids are annual garden plants. They are frequently grown indoors for their abundance of slipper-shaped, highly coloured flowers. Many hybrids can be found.

To encourage bloom:
Keep the plants cool and in bright light (but not direct sunlight). Water regularly to keep the soil moist.

- Good light
- Temp: 10-16°C (50-60°F)
- Keep moist and fed

Campanula isophylla
BELLFLOWER
FALLING STARS
ITALIAN BELLFLOWER
STAR-OF-BETHLEHEM
TRAILING CAMPANULA

Below: Stunning in a hanging basket, Campanula isophylla thrives in cool, airy conditions. Propagate by tip cuttings taken in early spring. This species should be pruned in autumn.

This exquisite plant is available in both pale blue and white colouring. The species is quite tough, but will be happier in lower temperatures, around 10°C (50°F), than it will be if grown in hot, stuffy rooms.

The leaves are small and pale green in colour and flowers are bell-shaped and produced continuously over a very long period from spring through into autumn. To encourage the maximum number of flowers, it is advisable to remove all dead flowers as soon as they appear.

Set off to best effect when grown in hanging baskets or containers, these plants will need frequent watering and ample feeding during spring and summer.

In the autumn when they are becoming more miserable in appearance they can be severely cut back, kept on the dry side, then repotted in the spring to start life all over again.

To encourage bloom:
Pinch off flowers as they fade.

- Good light
- Temp: 10-16°C (50-60°F)
- Keep moist, but dry in winter

Right: Delicate pink or white flowers (depending on the variety) adorn Catharanthus roseus during the summer months. The plant is best raised anew each year from seed or stem cuttings.

Catharanthus roseus
(Vinca rosea)
MADAGASCAR PERIWINKLE
ROSE PERIWINKLE
OLD MAID

This is a charming, trouble-free little plant that may be easily grown from seed sown in the spring or from tip cuttings taken at the same time of year. Cuttings of about 7.5cm (3in) in length should be taken from plants of the previous year and inserted in peat and sand mixture at a temperature of about 21°C (70°F).

Leaves are a bright glossy green and flowers may be either white or pink. It is really best to treat these as annuals so that fresh plants are raised in the spring each year and older plants discarded. A loam-based potting mixture will suit them best and once they have got under way it is advisable to remove the growing tips to encourage a more compact shape. They should be kept on a bright windowsill; while in active growth keep moist and feed with a weak liquid fertilizer at each watering.

To encourage bloom:
Raise new young plants. Feed well when growing actively.

□ Sunny location
□ Temp: 13-18°C (55-65°F)
□ Keep moist and fed

Celosia argentea
COCKSCOMB
PLUME CELOSIA
PRINCE OF WALES' FEATHERS

The variety *C. argentea* 'Cristata' is generally referred to as the 'cockscomb' because the bract it produces resembles the comb of the cockerel. The variety 'Pyramidalis' has plumed flowers in red or yellow. In any event, these are annual plants that are produced in large quantities both for indoor decoration in pots and for use as a bedding plant in the garden.

Over the years there have been many new varieties of this plant, but most have a somewhat

grotesque appearance and leave much to be desired, but they clearly have attraction for some indoor-plant growers. Cheapness has some bearing on *C. argentea's* popularity. Although it is discarded after flowering, the plant is very easily raised from seed sown in the spring. Seedlings are subsequently pricked off, and grown on in larger pots — the eventual size of pot dictating to some extent the dimensions of the mature plant.

To encourage bloom:
Keep cool and bright.

☐ Good light
☐ Temp: 10-16°C (50-60°F)
☐ Keep moist and fed

Below: This is the 'Cristata' variety of Celosia argentea, often referred to as the cockscomb. It is easily raised from seed and provides vivd colour.

Cineraria
(Senecio cruentus)

The compact, coarse green leaves and bright daisy flowers of this plant make it one of the most popular pot plants among the cheaper range. Ideally, seed should be sown in early spring and plantlets pricked off and potted on as they establish themselves.

Seed should be chosen wisely, and where growing space is limited the more miniature varieties should be selected. Seed of larger-growing types will develop into plants of splendid size in time if potted on and given regular feeding. A loam-based mixture is important as these are greedy plants that thrive on ample nourishment, both from the soil in which they are growing and from the subsequent feeding that they receive.

When raised in a greenhouse the cineraria can become the host for every pest that has ever been thought of, so inspect plants regularly and treat accordingly.

To encourage bloom:
Keep cool and fed.

☐ Good light
☐ Temp: 13-18°C (55-65°F)
☐ Keep moist and fed

Left: Cineraria is one of the finest gift plants. This well-known favourite has daisylike flowers in a spectrum of brilliant colours; well worth growing from seed if you want a challenge. Keep cool until buds form.

Euphorbia milii var. splendens
CHRIST PLANT
CHRIST THORN
CROWN OF THORNS

This delightful little shrub, only slightly succulent, is very popular as a houseplant, and deservedly so, as it is more suited to a well-lit living-room window in winter than to the average colder greenhouse, where it will certainly lose its long leaves, and probably its life also!

The plant's great attraction is its brilliant scarlet flower-like bracts, about 1.5cm (0.6in) across, produced freely in spring and summer. There is also a yellow version.

If the stems become too long, encourage more bushy growth by cutting them down to size; this also provides ample cuttings for spare plants. Keep any sap away from your eyes or mouth. Let the pieces dry for a few days and pot up; they should root fairly easily in spring and summer. Grow this euphorbia in any good loam- or peat-based potting mixture, and water freely in spring and summer.

To encourage bloom:
Provide full sunshine.

□ Full sun
□ Temp: 10-30°C (50-86°F)
□ Keep slightly moist in winter

Left: The stems of Euphorbia milii are covered in sharp prickles. Bright red bracts give this shrub great appeal. Avoid exposure to cold draughts in winter.

Above: Exacum affine is a one-season plant. A moist atmosphere will benefit its growth and picking off dead flowers keeps it blooming for longer.

Exacum affine
ARABIAN VIOLET
GERMAN VIOLET
PERSIAN VIOLET

In small pots on the windowsill there can be few prettier plants than *E. affine,* which has glossy green foliage and scented lavender-blue flowers. An added bonus is that, if old flowerheads are removed, the plant will continue in flower for many months from midsummer onwards.

In common with almost all flowering plants this one should have a very light location in which to grow. But very strong sunlight must be avoided, particularly when it is being magnified by window panes. Besides being a good individual plant *E. affine* is an excellent subject for including in mixed plant arrangements. Keep established plants moist and fed. New plants should be raised annually from seed.

New varieties with bright blue and with white flowers are available, so extending the colour range of this delightful plant.

To encourage bloom:
Keep plants humid and brightly lit, and pick off flowers as they fade.

☐ Good light
☐ Temp: 13-18°C (55-65°F)
☐ Keep moist and fed

Above: Hippeastrum hybrids are glorious bulbs which can be brought into bloom every year with a little care. Keep them slightly potbound and repot them every three or four years.

Hippeastrum hybrids
AMARYLLIS

Production of high-quality hippeastrum bulbs is one of the great skills of the more specialized commercial growers. But once matured, and in good light, these bulbs will produce their exotic trumpet flowers in a range of many colours. These are carried on stout stems 90cm (3ft) or more in height.

Bulbs can be purchased complete with their pots and growing soil and simply require the addition of water to start them growing. They should be kept moist but not excessively wet. However, problems can arise in subsequent years as not everyone can manage to get these plants to flower a second time. It helps to continue to feed the bulb and leaves after flowering until such time as the foliage dies down naturally, when the soil should be dried out and the plant stored cool and dry for the winter.

To encourage bloom:
Grow in bright light when active. Observe rest period.

□ Good light
□ Temp: 13-18°C (55-65°F)
□ Keep moist: dry winter rest

Hypocyrta glabra
CLOG PLANT

With so many plants to choose from, the glossy green succulent foliage and curiously shaped orange flowers make the hypocyrta an excellent plant for rooms offering limited space. Plants can be grown conventionally in pots on the windowsill, or they may be placed in smaller hanging containers. As hanging plants the generally drier conditions that prevail will suit hypocyrtas as they are capable of storing a considerable amount of water in their attractive puffy leaves.

Temperatures in the range 16-21°C (60-70°F) will suit them fine, as will a watering programme that errs on the side of dry rather than wet. These are hungry plants, but an occasional feed will keep them in good trim and help to retain their bright green colouring. New plants can be raised from stem cuttings.

To encourage bloom:
Do not overwater.

□ Light shade
□ Temp: 16-21°C (60-70°F)
□ Keep just moist; drier in winter

Left: Hypocyrta glabra is known for its goldfish shaped orange flowers. Hypocyrtas are compact plants; the leathery shiny leaves of this species make it handsome even when not in bloom.

Kalanchoe blossfeldiana
FLAMING KATY
TOM THUMB

This succulent is undoubtedly a houseplant, although it can certainly be grown in a greenhouse. Many horticultural hybrids are on the market, as they are popular florists' plants, usually being available in autumn and winter in full bloom. A typical specimen would be up to 30cm (12in) high with wide, thick bright green leaves, but the plants offered for sale are usually smaller. This is predominantly a flowering plant, producing masses of bright red flowers from autumn until spring. The flowers are individually small, but they are clustered in tight heads, giving a brilliant display of colour. There is a yellow-flowered variety.

Never overwater this plant, as the stems are prone to rot off, but never let it dry out completely either. However, in a good, well-drained potting mixture it is easy to cultivate; mix some extra sharp sand or perlite with a standard material to improve the drainage. Take stem cuttings in spring; pot them straight away.

To encourage bloom:
Provide really bright conditions.

- ☐ Good light
- ☐ Temp: 10-27°C (50-81°F)
- ☐ Keep slightly moist in winter

Schizocentron elegans
(Heterocentron)
SPANISH SHAWL

This compact windowsill plant is ideal for the beginner wishing to have something easy to keep in flower. Neat mounds of green foliage are topped by purplish flowers that are in evidence through the spring and into early summer.

Schizocentron elegans is best kept in a smaller pot using a loam-based potting mixture, but a keen eye must be maintained for watering and feeding, as smaller pots tend to dry out more rapidly. While actively growing, plants should be fed at every watering

with a weak liquid fertilizer. Alternatively, feeding tablets may be placed in the soil as directed by the manufacturer.

New plants can be produced in the autumn by cutting back the foliage of older plants to little more than stumps, then dividing the roots. Alternatively, tip cuttings about 7.5cm (3in) long can be taken at any time and rooted in a mixture of peat and sand.

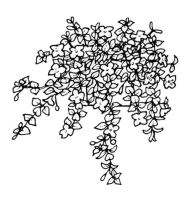

To encourage bloom:
Provide bright light all year.

☐ Good light
☐ Temp: 16-21°C (60-70°F)
☐ Keep moist and fed

Below: Kalanchoe blossfeldiana produces masses of brilliant flowers from autumn to spring. It is well-known as a houseplant and easy to restart from cuttings.

Zephyranthes candida
SWAMP LILY
ZEPHYR FLOWER

These bulbs are usually planted as outdoor subjects, where they thrive in well-drained loam in full sun. With care, they can be raised indoors, too. This species produces shining white, crocus-like flowers during late summer; pink and orange varieties are also available.

Place 4 or 5 bulbs in a 15cm (6in) pot in spring and cover them with a free-draining potting mix made up of equal parts of loam and peat. Keep the pot in a sunny window and water generously, allowing the soil to dry out between waterings. Feeding is not necessary.

When flowering is over, gradually reduce watering until the leaves die down completely. Store the dry bulbs in a cool, shaded place during the winter months, ready for planting up again the following spring.

Propagate *Zephyranthes* by detaching the offset bulbs that develop beside the main bulb.

To encourage bloom:
Provide bright conditions.

□ Good light
□ Temp: 16-21°C (60-70°F)
□ Keep moist; dry in winter

Right: Zephyranthes candida is a pretty plant that bears graceful white flowers in late summer and autumn. Pink flowering species of Zephyranthes are also available.

Moderately Easy to Grow

Most houseplant enthusiasts should have little difficulty in growing the plants in this section. Many are flowering houseplants which create colour for part of the year, then rest or have their growing stage and burst into flower the following year. These plants — often shrub-like and some eventually quite large — usually need careful watering during their dormant period. They include the golden trumpet (*Allamanda cathartica*), paper flower (*Bougainvillea*), Chinese rose (*Hibiscus rosa-sinensis*), pink jasmine (*Jasminum polyanthum*) and wax flower (*Stephanotis floribunda*).

Keeping plants from year to year is often easier if a conservatory or greenhouse is available. Indoors, where space is limited, non-flowering plants may prove difficult to accommodate.

Aechmea chantinii
AMAZONIAN ZEBRA PLANT

Allamanda cathartica
COMMON ALLAMANDA
GOLDEN TRUMPET

Among the bromeliads this one has a reputation for being tough. It has very vicious spines along the leaf margins, which makes careful handling, and positioning, essential. The green-and-silver banded foliage itself makes a striking plant, but when the red-and-orange coloured bract appears one begins fully to appreciate the spectacle that this splendid plant displays.

Like all the more majestic plants in the bromeliad family, this will take several years to produce bracts following the purchase of a young plant. New plants can be started from offshoots that appear at the base of the parent stems of an older plant that has produced bracts. These should be planted individually in a loam-based potting mixture to which some prepared tree bark has been added. Pot as firmly as possible to prevent the plants toppling over, and keep out of direct sunlight until new growth is evident.

To encourage bloom:
Keep in bright light.

□ Good light
□ Temp: 13-18°C (55-65°F)
□ Avoid overwatering

The allamanda is better suited to the conservatory or sunroom than indoors. Using a loam-based potting compost this rapid grower will require ample moisture at its roots and frequent feeding while in active growth in spring and summer.

For best effect, train the active growth as it develops to a framework of some kind so that when the golden-yellow trumpet flowers appear they are set off to maximum effect. Although the flowers are sometimes sparse, there will generally be more of them if the plants are fed with a fertilizer recommended for flowering plants — something with a fairly high potash content, rather than nitrogen.

In winter, the amount of water given can be reduced and the plants can be severely pruned back to create a better shape and more manageable size.

To encourage bloom:
Keep in sunny conditions and repot each year into the next pot size.

□ Good light
□ Temp: 16-21°C (60-70°F)
□ Keep moist and fed

Left: The stunning yellow flowers of Allamanda cathartica give this species its common name of golden trumpet. Grow the plant trained to a framework.

Aphelandra squarrosa 'Louisae'
SAFFRON SPIKE
ZEBRA PLANT

The aphelandra has two fairly obvious common names 'zebra plant' and 'saffron spike', relating to different parts of the plant — one to the grey-green leaves striped with silver, and the other to the saffron-yellow spike that forms the bract produced in midsummer. It is equally attractive with or without flowers, and reaches a height of about 60cm (2ft) when grown in a 13cm (5in) diameter pot. Larger pots will produce taller plants, usually in their second year.

When in good health all aphelandras will produce a wealth of roots and, consequently, require frequent feeding and potting on as soon as they have filled their existing pots with roots. Peaty mixtures are not much use to this plant; try a proprietary brand potting soil that contains a good proportion of loam. In spring and summer established plants must be fed with every watering.

To encourage bloom:
Rest after flowering.

☐ Light shade
☐ Temp: 16-21°C (60-70°F)
☐ Keep moist and fed

Above: Aphelandra squarrosa 'Louisae' is a colourful plant with striped leaves. Prune in spring to prevent legginess and avoid dry soil, which causes leaf drop.

Right: Azalea indica is a plant that can brighten any autumn day. A compact shrub, it can be in flower at Christmas. Cool conditions suit it best.

Azalea indica
(Rhododendron simsii)
INDIAN AZALEA

For a colourful display there is little that can match these plants when they are well grown. With its evergreen foliage and flowers in many colours, the azalea will be more attractive and last very much longer if given cool and light conditions indoors — hot conditions definitely shorten the life of the flowers. The most sensible way of watering is to grasp the pot in both hands and plunge it in a bucket of water and leave it submerged until every vestige of air has escaped from the soil. Depending on conditions, it may be necessary to repeat this exercise two or three times weekly during the spring and summer months, with only slightly less water being given in winter.

Remove dead flowers as they occur and place plants out in the garden for the summer, being sure to bring them in before frosts occur. Use a mix of peat and well-rotted leaves when potting on.

To encourage bloom:
Keep cool and light.

☐ Good light
☐ Temp: 10-16°C (50-60°F)
☐ Keep very moist

Begonia coccinea 'Orange Rubra'
ANGELWING BEGONIA

With glossy green leaves and lovely orange-coloured flowers this is one of the taller growing fibrous-rooted begonias (sometimes referred to as cane-type begonias). *Begonia* 'Orange Rubra' is only one example of the many cane-type begonias to be seen in florists and nurseries, and will offer a splendid show when in flower.

As the plants age they will have a natural tendency to shed their lower leaves, which will result in less attractive, bare stems, and this is one very good reason for raising fresh plants from easily rooted cuttings at regular intervals. Cuttings with three or four firm leaves can be taken at almost any time if a heated propagating case is available. Use rooting powder on the severed end of the cutting before inserting it in peat with a little sand added. When potting cuttings on it is advisable to put several cuttings in a pot for a fuller and more attractive display.

To encourage bloom:
Keep in a humid but not stuffy atmosphere.

☐ Filtered light
☐ Temp: 16-21°C (60-70°F)
☐ Keep moist and fed

Above: Bougainvillea is a popular red or purple flowering climbing plant, perfect for the sunny window. With careful culture, it will bloom freely throughout the summer. It benefits from a support.

Bougainvillea
PAPER FLOWER

Few flowering plants are capable of giving a display that equals that of the paper-thin bracts of the bougainvillea, particularly when seen in its natural tropical habitat.

In pots they can be more difficult to manage if the owner is someone who is forever watering. These plants should be well watered and allowed to dry reasonably before repeating, and when the foliage turns colour and drops in the autumn it is a sign that water should be withheld until the following early spring when new growth appears and watering can begin again. Pruning — it tolerates quite severe cutting back — can be done in the autumn. Repotting can be undertaken in spring, and is best done by removing some of the old soil and potting the plant into the same container with a fresh loam-based mixture. During the summer months fresh air and full sunlight are essential.

To encourage bloom:
Provide several hours sunshine a day during summer.

☐ Sunny location
☐ Temp: 13-18°C (55-65°F)
☐ Keep dry in winter

Left: Begonia 'Orange Rubra' is one of many tall fibrous-rooted begonias. It grows to a height of 90-120cm (3-4ft) and is festooned with drooping flowers.

Above: Many varieties of the beautiful Camellia japonica are available, all of which will bloom best in a cool conservatory. In summer, place the plant outside in a cool, shady spot.

Right: Clivia miniata produces superb flowers in early spring, but only if the plant has been given a dormant period of several weeks at the temperature of about 10°C (50°F) during late autumn.

Camellia japonica
COMMON CAMELLIA
TEA PLANT

These make fine garden plants in sheltered areas if the soil in which they are growing is acid rather than alkaline.

Perhaps not so good for the indoor location, they are nevertheless excellent plants for porches and conservatories that offer a little shelter from the elements. Plants that are grown from seed sown in the spring, or from cuttings rooted in the autumn, can be purchased in small pots from good retailers.

With careful handling these small plants can be gradually potted on until they are in containers of 25cm (10in) in diameter — use the acid soil recommended for camellias at each potting stage, and collect rain water for watering.

In time plants of about 150cm (5ft) in height will have developed, and in early spring there can surely be nothing more appealing than camellia blooms in white, pink or red.

To encourage bloom:
Maintain cool conditions.

□ Good light
□ Temp: 10-16°C (50-60°F)
□ Keep moist with rain water

Clivia miniata
KAFFIR LILY

To encourage these plants to flower freely, keep their roots in potbound condition — not a very difficult task as they very quickly make sufficient roots to fill existing containers. Getting these plants to produce their exotic orange bell-flowers is always a problem, but older plants will usually reward the patience expended on them in the end.

Leaves are thick, broad, and strap-like and are produced from very large bulbous stems at soil level. Clean leaves with a damp cloth to keep them looking their best. Inevitably, plants will require quite large pots as they mature, and when potting on it is advisable to use a loam-based mixture that will sustain the plant over a longer period of time.

Having outgrown their pots and perhaps their allotted space indoors, the bulbous clumps can be divided to make new plants.

To encourage bloom:
Grow slightly potbound and keep dry during winter rest.

☐ Shade
☐ Temp: 16-21°C (60-70°F)
☐ Keep moist

Cuphea ignea
CIGAR FLOWER
FIRECRACKER FLOWER
MEXICAN CIGAR PLANT
RED-WHITE-AND-BLUE FLOWER

This is a straggly plant with a mass of tiny leaves pin-pointed with an abundance of red tubular flowers. The ends of the tubular flowers are lipped with blackish-

Above: Cuphea ignea is an ideal plant for a brightly lit place. Young plants carry the most flowers so it is best to start or buy new ones each year.

Cyclamen persicum
ALPINE VIOLET
POOR MAN'S ORCHID
SHOOTING STAR
SOURBREAD

grey colouring not unlike cigar ash — hence the appropriate common name of 'cigar flower'.

New plants can be raised from seed sown in the spring or from stem cuttings taken in late summer. When only one or two plants are required it is usually better to purchase established plants, so saving the bother of overwintering or raising seed plants.

When in flower, cupheas are easy to manage on a light windowsill, needing no particular attention other than the usual watering and feeding. Once established in 13cm (5in) pots no further potting is needed, as plants will tend to become too large. Discard after flowering.

To encourage bloom:
Provide bright light.

□ Good light
□ Temp: 10-16°C (50-60°F)
□ Keep moist and fed

Ever popular, the cyclamen has a cool beauty that is matched by few other plants. Centrally heated rooms kept at excessively high temperature can be its worst enemy. On a cool windowsill that offers good light, the life of the cyclamen indoors will be much extended.

Water well by pouring water on to the soil surface and ensuring that surplus water is seen to drain through the holes in the bottom of the pot; repeat only when the foliage feels limps to the touch. But never allow leaves and flowers to flag excessively.

Clear out dead flowers and leaves complete with their stems to prevent rotting. Following flowering, plants die back naturally and should be stored cool and dry until new growth is evident — which is also the time to pot on.

To encourage bloom:
Give plenty of water. Keep the plants cool and humid (but do not spray the flowers). Give resting period.

□ Good light
□ Temp: 10-16°C (50-60°F)
□ Keep moist, but dry after flowering

Left: Cyclamen grow wild in Greece and along the eastern shores of the Mediterranean. Hybrids from these are highly prized indoor flowering plants.

Euphorbiá fulgens
SCARLET PLUME

This is an untidy sort of plant that produces small but brilliantly coloured scarlet flowers in early spring — a good time for indoor flowering plants when there is so little colour around. Like the more common *E. pulcherrima* (poinsettia) the bright scarlet flower is in fact a bract that surrounds the smaller and insignificant central flowers.

New plants can be grown from tip cuttings about 10cm (4in) in length, which should be inserted in clean peat moss and kept at a temperature not less than 21°C (70°F). The sap of this euphorbia can cause skin irritation, so gloves must be worn when the stem of the plant is being cut. Feed occasionally. Avoid both wet and cold conditions.

Plants will grow to a height of about 120cm (4ft) in ideal conditions. Check regularly for mealy bugs which may infest this plant if it is grown in too dry an atmosphere.

To encourage bloom:
Keep plant in bright light.

□ Good light
□ Temp: 16-21°C (60-70°F)
□ Keep on the dry side

Right: One of the most popular houseplants for winter colour is Euphorbia pulcherrima. This photograph shows several individual plants grouped together.

Euphorbia pulcherrima

CHRISTMAS FLOWER
CHRISTMAS STAR
MEXICAN FLAME LEAF
LOBSTER PLANT
PAINTED LEAF
POINSETTIA

This plant with its bright red, creamy green, or pink-coloured bracts is by far the finest of all winter-flowering indoor plants. The end of autumn to early winter is their natural flowering time and, given reasonable care, they will continue in colour for many months.

Avoid temperatures below 16°C (60°F) and be careful to water plants and allow them to dry reasonably before repeating. Feeding should never be to excess — weak liquid fertilizer can be given each week, and this should be sufficient for most plants.

To get plants to flower for a second year indoors ensure that only natural daylight is made available from early autumn until early winter. When not in flower, prune to shape.

Tip cuttings can be taken from new side-shoots after the bracts have dropped. Wash the poisonous latex from the cut end and insert an equal mix of peat and sharp sand.

To encourage bloom:
Be sure a dark period is given.

□ Good light
□ Temp: 16-21°C (60-70°F)
□ Keep moist and fed

Freesia

Among the most fragrant of all flowers the freesias are available in many wonderful colours, and will fill the entire room with their scent. The small bulbs belong to the iris family, and should be planted in loam-based houseplant soil in the autumn. Plant just below the soil surface and place bulbs almost touching in a shallow pot about 18cm (7in) in diameter. Pots are then placed in a cool, sheltered place (an unheated greenhouse, for example) in good light to establish. Once under way they can be transferred to a warmer location to develop their flowers, and placed on a light and cool windowsill indoors when blooms are present. Freesias are excellent as cut flowers, too.

Keep moist while in leaf; feeding is not normally necessary as bulbs are planted in fresh soil each autumn. Dry off and store bulbs after flowering.

To encourage bloom:
Keep cool and brightly lit.

☐ Good light
☐ Temp: 10-16°C (50-60°F)
☐ Moist; dry in winter

Above: Gloriosa rothschildiana is a fine tuberous plant with narrow leaves and orange, crimson and yellow flowers in summer.

Below: Available in many different colours, the graceful flowers of Freesia are exquisitely scented. Beautiful for indoor display.

Gloriosa rothschildiana
GLORIOSA LILY
GLORY LILY

These showy plants have glossy leaves and upright habit. They produce a wealth of exotic flowers during the summer months in orange and crimson with a yellow edge.

Plants should be started from tubers; these should go into an 11.5cm (4.5in) pot in peaty soil and later be transferred to pots of about 18cm (7in) in diameter when the smaller pots are well filled with roots. Use a loam-based mixture at this stage and put at least three of the contents of the smaller pots into the larger one, so that a good show is provided when the plant comes into flower.

It is also wise to place three or four 150cm (5ft) canes around the edge of the pot to which plants can be tied as they develop. Rest tubers during winter in a cool dry place.

To encourage bloom:
Keep plants moist when growing actively but be sure to provide dry dormant period.

- Good light
- Temp: 13-18°C (55-65°F)
- Keep moist, but dry when dormant

Guzmania lingulata
ORANGE STAR
SCARLET STAR

Belonging to the fine bromeliad family, there are a number of guzmanias that can be found in the quest for new plants to add to the houseplant collection, and all of them should prove moderately easy to manage.

The growing habit is that of most bromeliads — the plant forms a stiff rosette of leaves that protrudes from a short and stout central trunk. Overlapping leaves make a natural watertight urn, which must be kept filled with water. However, it is advisable to empty the urn and refill with fresh water periodically. Rain water is preferred but try to avoid getting the soil in the pot too wet. Impressive orange-scarlet bracts develop on short stems from the centre of the urn during winter. New plants can be started from offsets.

Bromeliads should be grown in a free-draining mixture; equal parts of a loam-based medium and peat will be ideal. Alternatively, use a prepared bromeliad mix.

To encourage bloom:
Grow in bright filtered light.

□ Good light
□ Temp: 13-18°C (55-65°F)
□ Keep on the dry side

Left: The beautiful yellow flowers and bright red stamens of Hedychium gardnerianum are produced during the summer months. This plant needs warmth and sunlight.

Hedychium gardnerianum
GARLAND LILY
GRUGER LILY
KAHLI GINGER

These plants of the ginger family (Zingiberaceae) can be grown by dividing the rhizomes in the spring and planting them independently. Once under way plants will grow apace and in time will require containers of about 25cm (10in) diameter. Once established, these plants need regular feeding. Lemon-yellow flowers are produced in summer on stems that may be 120cm (4ft) or more in length. Immediately after flowering, these stems should be cut down.

Where the climate permits, the plants in their pots can be placed out of doors during the summer months. They make excellent terrace plants when in decorative containers. Water freely in summer, but plants must be brought indoors before the weather turns cold and wet.

To encourage bloom:
Provide plenty of sunshine and always keep the plants moist and well fed.

□ Good light
□ Temp: 16-21°C (60-70°F)
□ Keep moist, and feed well

47

*Above: Depending on variety,
Hibiscus rosa-sinensis produces
large, showy flowers in red,
orange, pink, yellow or white.
Many grow and bloom indoors.
Take tip cuttings for propagation.*

Hibiscus rosa-sinensis

CHINESE HIBISCUS
CHINESE ROSE
GIANT MALLOW
ROSE MALLOW

These shrubby plants are widely dispersed throughout the tropics. They make fine indoor plants for the very light window location. Special growth-depressing chemicals are used to keep the plants short and compact, and to induce abundant blooms.

Trumpet flowers in numerous colours remain open for only a single day, but they are constantly being renewed from new buds during the summer months. It is important that plants have the best possible light and that

Ixia hybrids
CORN LILY
GRASS LILY

The hybrids of *Ixia* come in many delightful colours that will brighten any windowsill. Flowers are fragrant and carried on slender stems.

For a full and pleasing effect try planting five bulbs in a well-draining, loam-based mixture in 13cm (5in) diameter pots in late autumn. Plant the bulbs 7.5cm (3in) deep and place the pots in a dark, cool place until growth is evident. The pots can then be transferred to a cool windowsill indoors. Feeding is not necessary, but the soil must be kept moist, with care being taken to avoid saturation over long periods.

When the foliage begins to die back naturally, cease watering and store the bulbs in a dry, frost-free place until the next season. Do not try planting in the garden; ixias are not hardy out of doors in most temperate climates.

To encourage bloom:
Grow cool and bright once the plants are active.

□ Good light
□ Temp: 10-16°C (50-60°F)
□ Keep moist; give winter rest

the soil does not dry out during spring and summer; less water is required in winter.

Harsh pruning is not necessary with this species, but in the autumn plants may be trimmed back to better shape. In the spring, when new growth is evident, pot the plants on into slightly larger containers. Use a loam-based mixture for best results.

To encourage bloom:
Keep in constant temperature; sudden changes may cause buds to drop. Provide ample sunshine.

□ Sunny location
□ Temp: 13-18°C (55-65°F)
□ Keep moist and fed

Ixora coccinea
FLAME OF THE WOODS
INDIAN JASMINE
JUNGLE-FLAME
JUNGLE GERANIUM

As the name suggests, *Ixora coccinea* has brilliant red flowers, but there are also many other colours. All varieties are robust plants growing to a height of about 90cm (3ft).

While in active growth these plants will need regular feeding,

Left: Jasminum polyanthum is a splendid climbing plant from China with fragrant white and pale pink flowers. It needs support for good display.

Jasminum polyanthum
PINK JASMINE

Left: Ixora 'Peter Rapsley' is an undemanding plant with upright growth, bright green rounded leaves, and beautiful clusters of red flowers in early summer. Give this plant sunlight and humidity.

but none in winter. The same with watering — ample when plants are in growth, but very little over the winter period. In common with most flowering pot plants these will need a light location in order to obtain the maximum numbers of flowers.

New plants can be grown from cuttings 7.5-10cm (3-4in) long taken in spring and placed in fresh peat at a temperature of about 18°C (65°F). At all stages of potting a proprietary potting mixture is important. It is also essential to ensure that the soil is well drained. Pruning to shape can be done in early spring.

To encourage bloom:
Grow in warm, moist conditions without sudden changes.

□ Good light
□ Temp: 16-21°C (60-76°F)
□ Keep moist; drier in winter

This climbing plant produces rampant growth in ideal conditions and must have some sort of framework for the spiralling growth to wind around. In winter, plants must be kept in the coolest possible place and will tolerate being out of doors if frosts are not expected.

New plants can be raised very easily from summer-struck cuttings, several cuttings going into a 13cm (5in) pot after they have been rooted in pans or boxes of peat. Use loam-based potting mix, putting the more robust plants in time into 18cm (7in) pots. Provide a fan-shaped framework in the pot so that foliage is well spread, which will in turn display the flowers to best effect when they appear.

The flowers are more white than pink in colour, but the unopened buds are a delicate shade of pink. Feed and water well while active.

To encourage bloom:
Grow cool and bright.

□ Good light, some sunshine
□ Temp: 10-16°C (50-60°F)
□ Keep moist and fed

Lilium auratum
GOLD-BANDED LILY
GOLDEN-RAYED LILY
MOUNTAIN LILY

These are not the easiest of plants to manage indoors if they are used as permanent subjects, but they are excellent as temporary plants brought indoors when in bloom.

Bulbs are ready for planting in the autumn and should be planted about half way down a 20cm (8in) pot filled with lime-free peaty mixture. After potting, place the plants in a sheltered spot outside (a cold frame, for example) and cover the pots with a 10-13cm (4-5in) layer of peat. When growth shows through, the plants can be taken into a cool room. Water moderately until the growth becomes more vigorous, then water more freely, using rain water for preference. Stems will require staking. These plants need repotting annually in fresh mixture.

To encourage bloom:
Start in shade and coolness, then grow cool and bright.

□ Good light, some sunshine
□ Temp: 10-16°C (50-60°F)
□ Keep moist; dry rest period

Above: The colourful tropical shrub, Nerium oleander, will grow to about 1.8m (6ft) high in a pot and will respond well to bright light in the home or greenhouse.

Nerium oleander
OLEANDER
ROSE BAY

This is a fine plant frequently seen in the tropics, and yet equally at home in agreeable conditions indoors. A light and sunny location is essential, and plants should be well watered in summer when in active growth — less is required in winter. The same rule applies with feeding: none in winter, but once or twice each week when producing new leaves.

The semi-double rose-coloured flowers are slightly pendulous, fragrant, and a joy to have about the house. Cuttings of non-flowering shoots can be taken at any time during the summer months. Prepare the cuttings about 13cm (5in) in length and insert them in peaty mixture in modest heat. Be sure to wear gloves when taking cuttings to prevent the sap getting on to your skin. This plant is extremely poisonous if any part of it is eaten. When potting use a loam-based mixture.

To encourage bloom:
Provide plants with as much sunlight as possible all year.

□ Sunny location
□ Temp: 13-21°C (55-70°F)
□ Keep moist and fed

Passiflora caerulea
PASSION FLOWER

This plant is a rampant grower that will need some form of support for the twining growth to attach itself to. Hardy out of doors in agreeable climates but, out or in, the plant will give a better show of flowers if the roots are confined to a small space. If allowed a free root run it will tend to produce masses of foliage at the expense of flowers.

Striking 7.5cm (3in) flowers intricately patterned in blue, white and purple appear in late summer and are followed by colourful orange-yellow fruits.

To do well this plant needs good light, ample watering while in active growth, and feeding with a fertilizer containing a high percentage of potash — a tomato food, for example. When potting is essential, use a loam-based mixture.

New plants can be raised from seed or cuttings in spring.

To encourage bloom:
Provide ample light. Do not use pots larger than 20cm (8in) across, otherwise stems and leaves develop at the expense of flowers.

☐ Sunny location
☐ Temp: 10-16°C (50-60°F)
☐ Keep moist and fed

Sinningia speciosa
GLOXINIA

T hese plants may be acquired as tubers to be grown on, as seed to be sown and reared, or as finished plants from the retailer. Whatever the choice, splendid plants can be owned and admired; they have large, soft green leaves and their trumpet flowers up to

7.5cm (3in) across are produced throughout the summer months. A rosette of leaves develops from the tuber to be topped by almost stemless flowers.

While in leaf plants must be fed only with a high nitrogen fertilizer, but change to a high potash one when flower buds appear. Good light is maybe the most important need of this plant when in flower. Remove dead flowers to encourage new ones. When foliage dies down naturally in early autumn, allow the standard potting mixture to dry completely and store the tuber in a dry and warm place during the winter months.

To encourage bloom:
Give high-potassium feed when buds form. Pick off faded flowers.

□ Good light
□ Temp: 13-18°C (55-65°F)
□ Keep moist; dry rest

Left: Known for its spectacular flowers of white, blue and purple, and its colourful fruits, Passiflora caerulea is a fine example of nature at her best.

Below: Many fine hybrids of Sinningia speciosa are available, all with trumpet-shaped blooms in violet, red or white, some marked in contrasting shades.

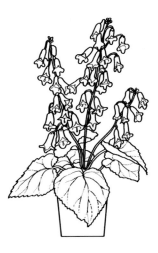

Smithiantha cinnabarina
TEMPLE BELLS

These interesting and colourful plants of the Gesneriaceae family can be kept in flower for many months of the year with a planned approach. Initially plants can be raised from seed or cuttings taken in the spring — keep the temperature at around 21°C (70°F) for both. Plants will grow and produce rhizomes and these can be planted at different times: spring planting for flowers in the autumn; and mid-summer planting for flowers in winter. If a heated greenhouse is available plants can be induced to flower over this extended season to much enhance the indoor plant scene. Once indoors avoid draughts and cold.

Lush green leaves are topped by bell-shaped flowers that are available in many colours. From a packet of seed one would expect to get a good selection of colours.

To encourage bloom:
Feed regularly when active. Observe dormant period.

□ Light shade
□ Temp: 16-21°C (60-70°F)
□ Keep moist and fed

Above: The bell-like flowers of Smithiantha cinnabarina appear in autumn and winter. They come in many colours.

Right: It is hard to beat the fragrance of Stephanotis floribunda, commonly known as Madagascar jasmine. White, star-shaped flowers appear in clusters in summer.

Stephanotis floribunda
FLORADORA
MADAGASCAR JASMINE
WAX FLOWER

Stephanotis will quickly fill its alloted space if given a free root run. Indoors, it requires a framework around which growth can be trained. Keep on the dry side in winter, and in the lightest possible location at all times, although avoiding direct summer sunshine.

The green, leathery leaves are evergreen and the flowers appear during the summer months. The white tubular flowers are produced in clusters of five or more and have the most overpowering scent.

Grow stephanotis in a loam-based mixture and repot into a slightly larger container every year. Feed with a standard liquid fertilizer every two weeks during the spring and summer and keep the soil and surrounding moist.

Pollinated flowers will occasionally result in large seedpots forming — these should be allowed to burst open before seed is removed and sown. New plants can also be grown from tip cuttings taken in spring.

To encourage bloom:
Keep in stable conditions.

☐ Good light
☐ Temp: 13-21°C (55-70°F)
☐ Keep moist; dry in winter

Streptocarpus hybrids
CAPE PRIMROSE
CAPE COWSLIP

In recent years, as with many other more common indoor plants, we have seen considerable improvement in the types of streptocarpus that are being offered for sale. Besides the more usual blue colouring of the variety 'Constant Nymph', there are now white, pink, red and purple shades available.

In culture they are all very similar, and require a light airy location at moderate temperatures to succeed. Place in good light with some protection from direct sunlight, and temperatures in the range 16-21°C (60-70°F). Feed every two weeks during the growing season with a high-phosphate fertilizer. Excessive watering can be damaging, so it is best to water the plant well and allow it to dry before repeating, bearing in mind that plants need much less water and no feed in winter.

New plants are raised by cutting leaves into 10cm (4in) sections and placing them in fresh peat at not less than 18°C (65°F).

To encourage bloom:
Remove seedpods as they form.

Above: If you want dazzling flowers, look to the Streptocarpus hybrids. Blooms come in shades of violet, pink or white. Allow plants to rest slightly after blooming.

☐ Good light
☐ Temp: 16-21°C (60-70°F)
☐ Do not overwater

Below: A bulbous plant from South Africa, Vallota speciosa is quite spectacular in full bloom. The scarlet flowers are produced in late summer.

Vallota speciosa
SCARBOROUGH LILY

Given reasonable light, moderate temperature, and care to prevent the potting mixture becoming excessively wet, these attractive plants will go on for years with few problems. The bulbous plants have green strap-shaped leaves and attractive scarlet flowers borne on stems about 60cm (2ft) in height.

New plants can be raised from seed or, perhaps more easily, from offsets that form around the base of the parent bulb. The offsets, which are very small, should be removed in the autumn for planting in a group in a shallow pan of peaty mixture. They do not need frequent repotting.

Unlike many bulbs, a resting period is not required, so the mixture — a rich, loam-based one is best — should be kept moist throughout the year. However, at no time should it become excessively wet.

To encourage bloom:
Provide plenty of sunshine.

□ Sunny location
□ Temp: 13-18°C (55-65°F)
□ Keep moist

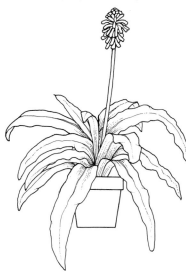

Veltheimia viridifolia
FOREST LILY

This bulbous plant from South Africa deserves to be more popular than it is at present. Leaves are large and soft green in colour. Its flowers — pink tinged with yellow — appear during the winter months.

Bulbs of *V. viridifolia* should be planted in early autumn to flower in winter. Place the bulbs in a loam-based mixture to which a liberal amount of peat has been added; just cover the bulbs with the mixture, ensuring that the potting is done with some firmness. Keep the soil on the dry side until new growth is under way, then water more liberally. Feed with a standard liquid fertilizer every month when in active growth.

They make good centrepiece plants provided they are given cool and light indoor conditions. During the summer place the plants in an unheated greenhouse until required again in the autumn.

To encourage bloom:
Observe summer rest period.

- □ Good light
- □ Temp: 16-21°C (60-70°F)
- □ Keep moist and fed

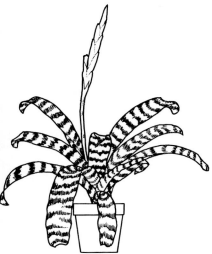

Above: The beautiful flower spike of Veltheimia viridifolia, which can grow to 60cm (2ft) tall, appears after the glossy, green leaves develop.

Vriesea splendens
FLAMING SWORD

This plant is a member of the bromeliad family with a typical rosette of overlapping leaves that form a natural urn for holding water. The urn must be kept topped up at all times but needs to be cleaned out and freshly watered.

The broad recurving leaves of *Vriesea splendens* are grey-green in colour with darker bands of brownish purple across the leaf. The flower spike usually develops in the summer and may last for many weeks. The bright red bracts enclosing the short-lived yellow flowers provide the main display.

Grow this plant in a mixture of equal parts of loam-based growing medium and fir bark chips, or use a commercially prepared bromeliad mix. The main rosette flowers only once then dies, but as the plant deteriorates offsets form at the base of the trunk and, once rooted, these can be detached and potted separately to provide new plants.

To encourage bloom:
Grow in bright light.

☐ Good light; some sunshine
☐ Temp: 16-21°C (60-70°F)
☐ Keep moist; drier in winter

Left: Vriesea splendens is a magnificent plant that needs high humidity to flourish. Feed once a month when it is active.

Difficult to Grow

As a general rule, any plant that is kept from year to year tends to present a challenge to the grower. Unlike those plants which are bought when bearing flowers and discarded after the display is over, those which live for several years usually demand different treatments both when in flower and afterwards during dormancy. For example, the plants may benefit from being placed in a greenhouse or conservatory during the period when they are not in bloom.

The majority of the plants in this section are shrub-like and, if properly cared for, should remain with you for a long time. Many of the more flamboyant cascading and trailing plants may prove particularly difficult to grow and flower. These include the lipstick vine (*Aeschynanthus lobbianus*) and the goldfish plants *(Columnea)*.

Acalypha hispida
CHENILLE PLANT
PHILIPPINE MEDUSA
RED HOT CAT'S TAIL

These striking plants, with their large leaves of mid-green colouring, grow to a height of some 1.8m (6ft) in ideal conditions. Drooping beetroot-red bracts develop from the axils of leaves to create the principal attraction of this fine plant.

The best time to purchase these plants is in the spring when the fresh young ones will get off to a better start. Keep them moist at all times, giving a little less water in winter, and feed well when they are established. When they have filled their existing containers with roots, use a loam-based potting compost to pot the plants on and help to develop them to their full potential.

Keep your acalypha in good light but avoid strong sunlight. Remove the dead bracts regularly and keep a watchful eye for pale leaf discolouration, which is a sign that troublesome red spider mites are present. Treat the undersides of leaves with insecticide promptly.

To encourage bloom:
Provide plenty of water and light.

□ Good light
□ Temp: 13-18°C (55-65°F)
□ Keep moist and fed

Left: At its best when young, Acalypha hispida is adorned in late summer with distinctive red catkins. It is beneficial to renew plants each year from cuttings.

Aeschynanthus lobbianus
BASKET VINE
BASKET PLANT
BLUSHWORT
LIPSTICK VINE

These are temperamental plants that will produce exotic red flowers with seeming abandon one year, and in spite of having had identical treatment, will produce very little the next year. One of the supposed secrets of getting them to flower more reliably is to keep the plants very much on the dry side in winter and to lower the growing temperature. It is a procedure that works for many of the similar gesneriads, such as the columneas. During the warmer months, they should be kept out of bright sunlight.

The plants have glossy green leaves and have a natural pendulous habit, which adds considerably to their charm. New plants are easily started from cuttings a few centimetres in length that may be taken at any time during the spring or summer months. Arrange several cuttings in a small pot filled with peaty mixture and this will ensure that full and attractive plants develop.

To encourage bloom:
Give dry winter rest.

□ Light shade
□ Temp: 16-21°C (60-70°F)
□ Keep moist and fed

Above: Anthurium scherzerianum appears almost artificial. The brilliant red spathes of anthuriums make them a popular indoor plant. Miniatures are available.

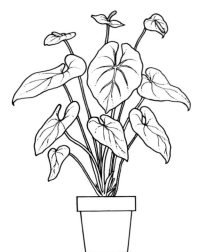

Anthurium andreanum
FLAMINGO FLOWER
FLAMINGO LILY
OILCLOTH FLOWER
PAINTERS' PALETTE

One of the most spectacular of all the flowering plants grown in pots, this needs a temperature in excess of 18°C (65°F) and a high degree of humidity to give of its best. Flowers may be pink, white or red, with the latter being the colour most frequently seen.

As cut flowers *A. andreanum* has no peers. Flowers are borne on long stalks and from the time they

Anthurium scherzerianum
FLAMINGO FLOWER
PIGTAIL PLANT
TAILFLOWER

This is the baby brother of *A. andreanum,* but is much better suited to average room conditions, in both space requirements and care. Green leaves are produced on short petioles from soil level, and flowers are generally red in colour and produced over a long spring and summer period. The spadix in the centre of the flower has a natural whorl to it that gives rise to one of its common names, 'pigtail plant'.

All anthuriums require an open potting mixture, and one made up of equal parts of peat and well-rotted leaves will be better than an entirely peat mix, or a mix containing loam. Once established, plants need regular feeding to maintain leaf colouring and to encourage production of flowers with stouter stems — weak-stemmed flowers will require support. Keep this plant out of direct sunlight.

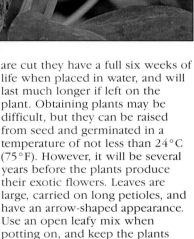

are cut they have a full six weeks of life when placed in water, and will last much longer if left on the plant. Obtaining plants may be difficult, but they can be raised from seed and germinated in a temperature of not less than 24°C (75°F). However, it will be several years before the plants produce their exotic flowers. Leaves are large, carried on long petioles, and have an arrow-shaped appearance. Use an open leafy mix when potting on, and keep the plants well watered, misted, and away from direct sunlight.

To encourage bloom:
Provide humid conditions.

□ Light shade
□ Temp: 18-24°C (65-75°F)
□ Keep moist and fed

To encourage bloom:
Provide humid conditions.

□ Light shade
□ Temp: 16-21°C (60-70°F)
□ Keep moist and fed

Beloperone guttata
FALSE HOP
MEXICAN SHRIMP PLANT
SHRIMP PLANT

The common name of 'shrimp plant' derives from the shrimp-like bracts that are freely produced on vigorous plants. On the more common 'shrimp plant', bracts are a dullish red in colour, but there is also *B. g. lutea,* which has interesting greenish yellow bracts.

Purchased plants should have their roots inspected immediately, and if a mass of roots is in evidence the plants must be potted without delay into a loam-based mixture. Failure to do so will mean leaf discolouration and a general decline of the plant. Regular feeding is also of the utmost importance, and avoid dank, airless conditions. Growing tips of young plants should be removed to encourage a more bushy appearance. And if one has the courage to do so it will strengthen young plants if all the early bracts that develop are removed.

To encourage bloom:
Prune rigorously each year for compact, free-flowering plants.

□ Light shade
□ Temp: 16-21°C (60-70°F)
□ Keep moist and fed

*Above: Bouvardia x domestica is a
desirable plant for the indoor
garden because of its colour
varieties; but it requires space.*

Bouvardia x domestica
JASMINE PLANT
TROMPETILLA

These compact, shrubby plants
produce flowers of many
colours on the end of slightly
drooping stems. They are ideal for
a window location that offers good
light and a modicum of fresh air,
but not necessarily cold
conditions. An added bonus with
the bouvardia is that it is autumn
flowering, so providing a display
when there are fewer flowering pot
plants around.

During the summer months
established plants will be better for
being placed out of doors in a
sheltered position — in colder
areas they will need the protection
of an unheated greenhouse.

Plants should be watered freely
and fed regularly during the
summer months, less water and no
feeding being required during
winter. Plants are best potted in the
spring, and a loam-based mixture
will suit them better than an all-
peat preparation. Spring is also the
time to take cuttings or divide the
roots.

To encourage bloom:
Pinch out growing tips in summer
for autumn bloom.

□ Light shade
□ Temp: 13-18°C (55-65°F)
□ Keep moist and fed

*Left: Flesh-coloured overlapping
bracts give Beloperone guttata its
common name of 'shrimp plant'. It
blooms most of the year.*

Browallia speciosa
BUSH VIOLET

The flower colouring of B. speciosa ranges from blue to violet-blue, but there are white varieties available. It should be reasonably easy to raise new plants from seed on the windowsill for the person who is moderately

Citrus mitis
(Citrofortunella mitis)
CALAMONDIN ORANGE

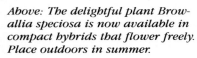

Above: The delightful plant Browallia speciosa is now available in compact hybrids that flower freely. Place outdoors in summer.

Left: Citrus mitis, the miniature orange tree, can produce a profusion of fruit if conditions are right. Needs plenty of sun.

competent with indoor plants. Sow seed in spring in peat to which a little sharp sand has been added, and after sowing just cover the seed with a fine layer of sand. Place a sheet of glass over the container holding the seed, and over the glass place a sheet of newspaper until the seed has germinated. When large enough to handle, the seedlings can be pricked off into a very peaty mixture with reasonable space for seedlings to develop. Subsequently, transfer the tiny plants to small pots filled with a loam-based mixture. From then on keep them moist, fed, and in good light. Discard the plants after they have flowered.

To encourage bloom:
Keep plants cool and fed during the summer months.

□ Good light
□ Temp: 13-18°C (55-65°F)
□ Keep moist and fed

Citrus mitis is one of the most decorative of potted plants when its branches are festooned with perfectly shaped miniature oranges. The glossy green foliage will become yellow if underfed, particularly from magnesium deficiency — to combat this deficiency treat with sequestered iron.

Full light is essential, but foliage may become scorched if plants are placed too close to window panes on very sunny days. During the summer months plants will do better if placed out of doors in full sun. While in the garden it is important not to neglect feeding and watering. Failure to keep the soil moist will result in shrivelling of leaves.

White, heavily scented flowers appear in late summer. To help with pollination draw your hands through the flowers periodically. Flowers are followed by small green fruits that will in time develop into miniature oranges — dozens of them!

To encourage bloom and fruit:
Put plants outdoors in the summer and keep them moist.

□ Sunny location
□ Temp: 13-18°C (55-65°F)
□ Keep moist and fed

Columnea banksii
GOLDFISH VINE

This much-neglected plant has many fine qualities, not least its abundance of attractive flowers and the fact that it is almost totally free of pests.

Evergreen, oval-shaped leaves are a dull green in colour and are attached to woody stems. Initially, the stems are supple and will hang naturally over the container in which the plant is growing, but in time they become rigid.

Besides the distinct advantage of being a natural hanging plant, this columnea will also oblige with a wealth of reddish-orange flowers in early spring when flowering houseplants are not so plentiful.

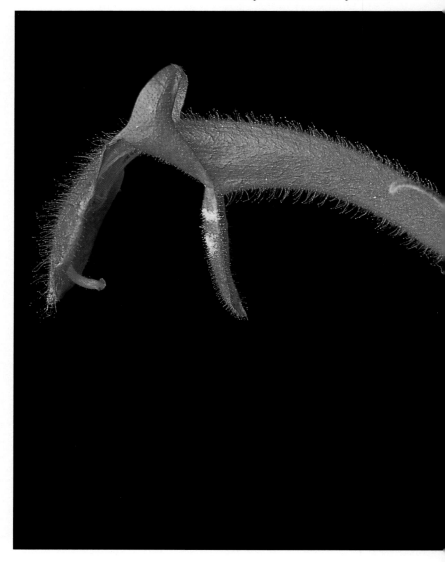

However, getting plants to produce their flowers can be a problem, but one way is to keep the soil very much on the dry side during winter and at the same time lower the growing temperature by several degrees. New plants are easily started from cuttings.

To encourage bloom:
Observe winter rest period.

□ Light shade
□ Temp: 16-21°C (60-70°F)
□ Keep moist, but drier in winter

Below: A mass of blooms in spring, Columnea banksii is ideal for basket growing. This plant is easy to propagate from cuttings.

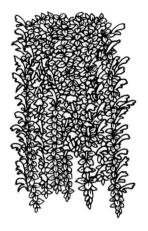

Columnea microphylla
GOLDFISH VINE

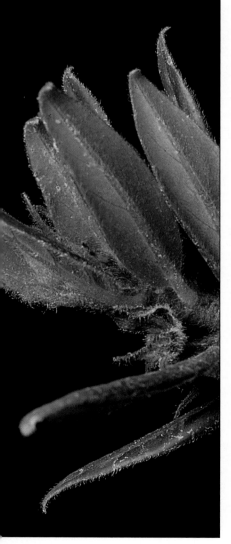

This is one of the more difficult columneas to grow successfully. The difficulty lies in the fact that it requires a constant temperature in the region of 18-21°C (65-70°F). Nevertheless, once the challenge is accepted, the results can be very rewarding. The small, oval-shaped, pale-green leaves are attached to wiry stems that hang perpendicularly from the container in which the plant is growing. Essentially, it is a hangng plant and can be seen at its best when provided with a hanging pot or basket in which to grow.

Flowers, generally produced during the summer months, are rich orange and red in colour and on mature plants are produced in great abudance. Something that adds to their attraction is that mature plants in large baskets may have trails 1.8m (6ft) or more in length, and may well have flowers from top to bottom.

It is important to keep the soil moist and to feed regularly with weak liquid fertilizer.

To encourage bloom:
Keep dry during winter.

□ Shade
□ Temp: 18-21°C (65-70°F)
□ Keep moist; drier in winter

Crossandra infundibuliformis
FIRECRACKER FLOWER

These are neat plants for the windowsill, needing light and airy conditions, with some protection from strong sunlight. The soil needs to be kept moist at all times, with less water being required in winter. In winter there will also be no need to feed plants, but while in active growth they will respond to feeding with weak liquid fertlizer. Vigorous plants will tolerate and benefit from feeding at every watering. An alternative to liquid feeding would be the use of tablet or stick-form fertilizers that are pressed into the soil and made available to the plant over a period of several weeks.

Naturally glossy green leaves are topped by bright orange flowers in the spring, with the possibility of further flowers later in the year. New plants can be started from seed or cuttings.

To encourage bloom:
Provide plants with good air circulation at all times.

☐ Good light
☐ Temp: 16-21°C (60-70°F)
☐ Keep moist

Above: From India and the East Indies, Crossandra infundibuli-formis boasts fine orange flowers at intervals during the year. It thrives on sun and humidity.

Right: Dipladenia splendens 'Rosea' is an elegant climbing plant that needs warmth and humidity to flourish and produce fine rose-pink flowers in summer.

Dipladenia splendens 'Rosea'
PINK ALLAMANDE

This is a natural climbing plant best suited to the heated conservatory or greenhouse, but a challenging plant that will be good for the ego of the houseplant-grower who cultivates it successfully. Indoors, it is best to confine the roots to pots of modest size so that growth is restricted. However, very small pots are often difficult to manage, so pots of 13cm (5in) diameter will be best.

For potting, use a loam-based mixture as opposed to a very peaty mix, which will tend to produce soft growth.

During the summer months healthy plants are festooned with attractive soft pink flowers, and these are the principal feature of the dipladenia. After flowering the plant can be pruned to shape, if needed.

The soil should be kept moist without being totally saturated for long periods, and regular feeding will be beneficial when growth is active.

To encourage bloom:
Keep in a sunny place.

☐ Good light
☐ Temp: 16-21°C (60-70°F)
☐ Keep moist and fed

Right: Although Episcia dianthiflora appears for only a short period during the summer, the fringed flowers of this basket plant are a delight to behold.

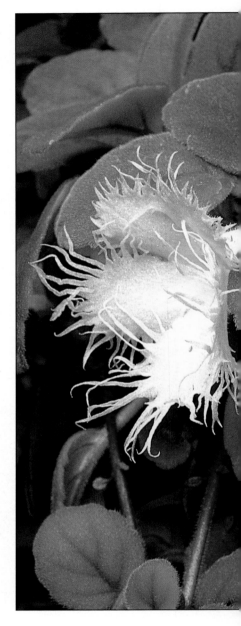

Episcia cupreata
CARPET PLANT
FLAME VIOLET
LOVEJOY

This is an attractive plant that grows in a pendulous fashion and looks good in small hanging pots. Leaves are an attractive greyish silver and green, and flowers, though small, are of brilliant red colouring and appear for many months in the middle of the year. Where growing conditions are to their liking, these plants can be grouped in hanging baskets of reasonable size to make a splendid feature in a room.

Good light is essential, but strong, direct sunlight should be avoided. In terms of temperature there is little to worry about in the summer, but the winter temperature should not drop below 16°C (60°F). Plants need to be potted with a peaty mixture.

In winter it is important to give water sparingly and only when it is really needed by the plant. Winter feeding is not necessary, but plants will benefit from regular applications at other times.

To encourage bloom:
Provide adequate humidity.

☐ Good indirect light
☐ Temp: 16-21°C (60-70°F)
☐ Keep on the dry side

Episcia dianthiflora
LACE FLOWER
LACE-FLOWER VINE

A delightful plant, *E. dianthiflora* has small rosettes of green leaves and produces mis-shapen tubular flowers, white in colour with lace-like, ragged edges to the petals. Growth hangs perpendicularly on stems that will become firm as they age, which makes this one of the best natural trailing plants for indoors.

Avoid excessively wet conditions; aim to give the potting mixture a good watering and allow it to dry quite appreciably before repeating. If plants are growing in hanging pots with drip trays attached it is important to empty these trays an hour or so after watering to ensure that the soil does not become too saturated. Feed established plants occasionally, but do not overdo it; pot on only when the plants are very well rooted. Raise new plants from the rosettes of leaves.

To encourage bloom:
Provide adequate humidity.

□ Light shade
□ Temp: 13-18°C (55-65°F)
□ Keep on the dry side

Gardenia jasminoides
CAPE JASMINE
COMMON GARDENIA

These are shrubby plants with small oval-shaped green leaves that will have a marked tendency to take on chlorotic yellow colouring if conditions are not to the liking of the plant. They are difficult plants to care for, needing a temperature of not less than 18°C (65°F), a lightly shaded location, and careful watering and feeding. Rain water is preferable to tap water and it will benefit plants if the foliage is misted over with water when the atmosphere tends to be dry. Frequent weak feeding will be better than giving occasional heavy doses. Use an acid-type fertilizer and pot the plants in an acid or peat-based mixture.

But, in spite of the problems, the gardenia is well worth trying to raise, as there are few flowers that can match its heavy, overpowering scent. Flowers are creamy white and up to 10cm (4in) across.

To encourage bloom:
Keep plants in constant warmth and high humidity as flower buds form.

□ Light shade, no sun
□ Temp: 18-21°C (65-70°F)
□ Keep moist

Left: The magnificent plant Gardenia jasminoides needs care to ensure that it flowers indoors. Sudden temperature changes will cause the flowers to drop. Keep the gardenia potbound.

Below: Haemanthus katharinae has a brilliant flower head of starry blooms that is produced in late spring. This beautiful bulbous plant resents disturbance, so repot only occasionally.

Haemanthus katharinae
AFRICAN BLOOD LILY
BLOOD FLOWER
BLOOD LILY
CATHARINE WHEEL

Haemanthus are grown from bulbs planted to a little over half their depth in a free-draining, loam-based potting mixture. To help with the drainage incorporate a good amount of sand and ensure that some drainage material — pot shards, for instance — is placed in the bottom of the pot before adding the mixture.

Water sparingly until green leathery leaves appear, then more freely, but never to excess. On stems about 30cm (12in) in length the plant bears globes of small orange-red flowers in late spring. Place single bulbs in pots of 13cm (5in) diameter and continue growing the plants in the same potting mixture for several years to get the best results. When foliage naturally colours at the end of the summer allow the soil to dry completely and store the bulb in a warm dry place.

To encourage bloom:
Grow in bright light when active and repot only when roots appear on the surface of the soil.

□ Good light
□ Temp: 16-21°C (60-70°F)
□ Keep moist, dry when dormant

Hoya australis
PORCELAIN FLOWER
WAX PLANT

WAX VINE

These attractive plants will climb or trail. To climb they will need a supporting frame, and to trail a hanging basket is ideal. The growing tips should be removed to encourage a bushy appearance. However, avoid unnecessary pruning as plants produce their flowers from older rather than new growth.

A loam-based, well-drained potting mixture should be used and the addition of a little charcoal when potting will prevent the mixture becoming sour. Remember to keep plants on the dry side during the winter.

New plants can be raised from stem cuttings taken from the previous year's growth and inserted in peat and sand at a temperature of about 21°C (70°F). Or, more simply, trailing pieces of stem can be pegged down during the summer and then cut from the parent plant and potted individually when they have rooted.

To encourage bloom:
Grow in bright light.

□ Good light
□ Temp: 16-21°C (60-70°F)
□ Keep moist and fed

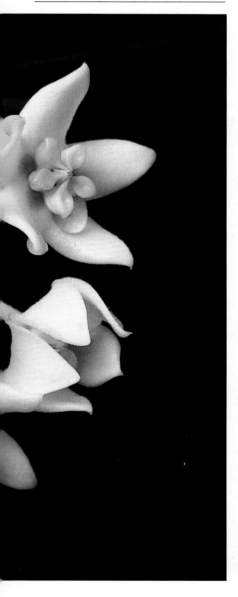

Hoya bella
MINIATURE WAX PLANT

When well established and in full bloom there can be few more rewarding plants than *Hoya bella* growing in a hanging container. The small pale green leaves are attached to wiry stems, but it is the flowers hanging in clusters that are the main attraction. Individual flowers have the appearance of exquisitely cut jewels, white in colour flushed with a delicate shade of pink.

For best results use a loam-based potting mixture that incorporates a reasonable amount of sand to ensure good drainage. If the hanging container is provided with a built-in drip tray, then check an hour or so after watering and tip away any surplus water in the tray. Also, check regularly for signs of mealy bug on the underside of leaves.

To encourage bloom:
Do not prune or move plants in bud. Give winter rest.

□ Light shade
□ Temp: 16-21°C (60-70°F)
□ Keep on the dry side

Left: Hoya australis has clusters of dainty white blooms which are waxy in texture. While actively growing, feed with a high-potassium liquid fertilizer.

Hoya carnosa
WAX PLANT

The twining stems and dark green leaves of this vigorous plant are quick to grow but the flowers that sprout from the leaf and stem joints are slow to appear. They are more likely to appear first on mature plants, but the clusters of pendulous pink jewels are well worth waiting for. As with all the hoyas, let the old flowers fall naturally and do not break off the flower stalks as these are the source of the following year's flowers.

This hoya makes a rather untidy basket plant, and is seen to best effect when trained to a framework of some kind. In this respect the plant is well suited to a heated conservatory, where growth can be trained overhead so that the flowers can be admired to full advantage when they appear. Well-draining, loam-based potting mixture is essential. Give frequent checks for mealy bugs in branches.

To encourage bloom:
Maintain good light as buds form.

☐ Good light
☐ Temp: 13-21°C (55-70°F)
☐ Keep moist and fed

Left: Jacobinia carnea is a handsome Brazilian plant with dark green leaves and plumes of pink flowers which appear in late summer for several weeks.

Above: Hoya carnosa is the most commonly grown in the Hoya genus. Be sure to give it sufficient room to grow; it needs a support as it climbs.

Jacobinia carnea
BRAZILIAN PLUME
KING'S CROWN

This attractive plant has pink flowers that bloom in late summer but there are other varieties occasionally available. Take cuttings of young shoots about 10cm (4in) in length in the spring, using fresh peat and a heated propagator to encourage rooting. Older plants should be cut down to the base after flowering and will flower in subsequent years, but it is often better, if space is limited, to produce new plants from cuttings and to discard the older plant.

While in active growth this vigorous plant will need regular feeding to retain leaf colouring, and ample watering. If an old plant is kept for the following year it will require no feed and little water during the winter. *Jacobinia carnea* is an ideal garden-room plant.

For mature plants use a loam-based potting mixture and repot regularly as the plant grows. Give a winter rest at about 13°C (55°F).

To encourage bloom:
Provide ample light. Take cuttings for vigorous young plants.

☐ Good light
☐ Temp: 16-21°C (60-70°F)
☐ Keep moist and fed

Kohleria amabilis
TREE GLOXINIA

Plant *Kohleria amabilis* in hanging containers suspended at head level to appreciate fully the attractive bright green foliage and to enjoy the flowers to the full when they appear in late spring and early summer.

However, encouraging plants to produce their attractive pink blooms is not easy. Moist soil, a humid atmosphere and a light position will all help flowering. A further encouragement would be the use of a houseplant food specifically recommended for flowering plants — one that has a fairly high potash content, as opposed to nitrogen. If special fertilizers are unobtainable, try one of the many fertilizers recommended for tomato plants.

Raise new plants by taking cuttings of young shoots in late spring, or by dividing the rhizomes in early spring. Use a peaty soil for potting.

To encourage bloom:
Grow warm and humid.

□ Good light
□ Temp: 16-21°C (60-70°F)
□ Keep moist and fed

Below: The beautiful flowers of the vining plant Lapageria rosea flourish in a cool, moist environment. Give the plant a supporting structure.

Lapageria rosea
CHILEAN BELLFLOWER
CHILE-BELLS
COPIHUE

Above: Keep Kohleria amabilis warm and moist while actively growing and it will produce lovely orange-pink flowers. Hybrids can bloom all year.

L*apageria rosea* can be a most rewarding plant to grow, providing all the right conditions can be met. In an ideal situation the plant will produce elegant funnel-shaped flowers that hang in the most graceful fashion. There are a number of colours available but many people feel that the original crimson form and the white-flowered variety make a stunning combination when grown together.

Grow in a lime-free potting mixture and use rain water when watering. Provide a framework either in the pot or against the wall for the foliage to climb through. Plants flower mainly in the summer and attain a height of about 4.5m (15ft). Provide good drainage and water with care, avoiding hot and dry conditions.

Prune lightly after flowering to take out weak growths. Propagate by seed sown in early spring or by layering strong shoots. Spray against aphids on young shoots.

To encourage bloom:
Maintain lime-free conditions.

□ Good light
□ Temp: 10-18°C (50-65°F)
□ Keep moist; drier in winter

Manettia bicolor
BRAZILIAN FIRECRACKER
CANDY CORN PLANT
FIRECRACKER PLANT
FIRECRACKER VINE
TWINING FIRECRACKER

To keep this plant under control requires a framework of some kind through which its twining growth can be trained. Depending on the shape wanted, taller supports can be provided for plants to climb.

New plants can be raised from spring-sown seed, or from cuttings of young growth taken in midsummer and kept warm. When potting, ensure that a liberal amount of sand and charcoal is incorporated in the mixture, which should be loam-based.

Water freely and feed frequently during the growing season, and moderately when growth slows up. Delightful tubular flowers — red with a yellow tip — appear throughout the summer months. Plants can be moderately pruned after they have flowered. During the summer *Manettia* will need protection from strong sunlight.

To encourage bloom:
Provide bright light all year round and keep plants moist and fed when growing actively.

☐ Good light
☐ Temp: 16-21°C (60-70°F)
☐ Keep moist and fed

Right: The vining plant Manettia bicolor will grow well indoors and produce yellow and scarlet tubular flowers in summer.

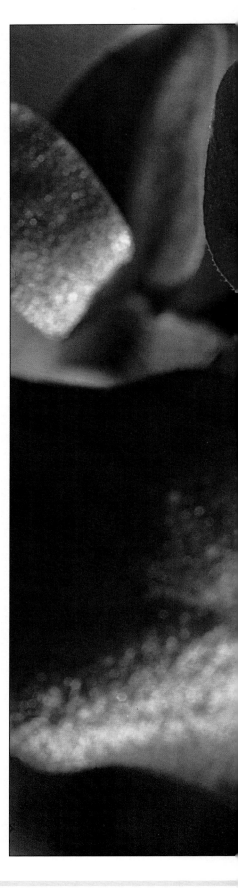

Medinilla magnifica
LOVE PLANT
ROSE GRAPE

Native to the Philippines, this plant will be a test for all who are interested in houseplants, but the reward of seeing pink flower clusters suspended from healthy plants will make all the effort worthwhile. Warm conditions, around 21°C (70°F), and a lightly shaded location are essential. Plants must be watered well throughout the year, with slightly less needed in winter.

Pendulous flowers may appear throughout the year, with summer being the most prolific time. The plants have square-shaped stems from which the flowers sprout and develop in the most amazing fashion. Use a loam-based potting mixture to which some peat and leaf mould have been added. To get the full effect of the pendulous flowers place the plant on a pedestal.

To encourage bloom:
Keep in humid conditions. Only mature plants will bloom.

- ☐ Light shade
- ☐ Temp: 18-24°C (65-75°F)
- ☐ Keep moist and fed

Left: The luxuriant plant Medinilla magnifica is best grown in a greenhouse, where warm, humid conditions can be maintained.

Pachystachys lutea
LOLLIPOP PLANT

This is a relative of the more familiar aphelandra, but has less vividly marked foliage — the pachystachys having simple mid-green, roughly lance-shaped leaves. However, where the pachystachys scores is in its much longer flowering period and in the fact that healthy plants will produce a far greater number of flowers. Flowers are erect in habit and a rich yellow in colour — or more correctly the bracts are rich yellow, the flowers produced from the bracts being white and tubular in appearance.

Success lies with light, water, and feeding. Avoid direct sun, but keep in the light, and water and feed well. No feeding and less water in winter. Repot annually in a loam-based potting mixture.

Take tip cuttings from the lower branches in spring, dipping the cut end in hormone rooting powder before placing the cuttings in a peat, moss and sand mix.

To encourage bloom:
Feed a high-potassium fertilizer.

- ☐ Good light
- ☐ Temp: 16-21°C (60-70°F)
- ☐ Keep moist and fed

Left: Pachystachys lutea is a shrubby plant with lance-shaped leaves and clearly marked veins. The overlapping yellow bracts protect the white tubular flowers.

Pentas lanceolata
EGYPTIAN STAR CLUSTER
EGYPTIAN STAR FLOWER
STAR CLUSTER

Though not often supplied by growers, this is a fine plant that can be seen in better plant collections. Plants can be started from new shoots about 10cm (4in) in length taken in the spring and placed in a peaty mixture — a warm propagating case will encourage rooting. Once rooted well, the small pots of cuttings should be transferred to slightly larger pots. Place drainage material in the bottom of the new pot before adding loam-based mixture and some grit for improved drainage.

As they develop, remove the growing tips of the young plants. This will encourage a compact habit and prevent the plants growing too tall. Keep the plants in good light and feed regularly and water well while actively growing.

These plants normally flower from early autumn until midwinter, but blooms can appear during the summer months as well.

To encourage bloom:
Maintain bright light throughout the year and allow plants to become slightly potbound.

□ Good light
□ Temp: 16-21°C (60-70°F)
□ Keep moist and fed

Left: Bright clusters of flowers appear on Pentas lanceolata during autumn and winter. Colours are available in magenta, pink, lavender and white.

Above: In warm, humid surroundings, Rechsteineria cardinalis will bear clusters of tubular red flowers for many weeks in summer. The plant grows from a rhizome.

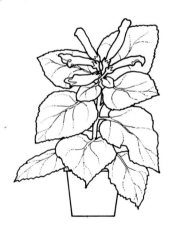

Rechsteineria cardinalis
CARDINAL FLOWER

This species is a gesneriad with green velvety leaves that produces flowers of bright red colouring in the summer months. For a neat plant that provides colour for many weeks, *Rechsteineria cardinalis* (also known as *Sinningia cardinalis*) can be thoroughly recommended.

A temperature of not less than 18°C (65°F) is needed and water must be tepid rather than straight from a cold tap. Exposure to bright light will leach the colouring from foliage and mar the appearance of the plant, so place in light shade. Keep the plant out of draughts.

Water well and feed occasionally during spring and summer when plants are in leaf, but when the foliage dies back naturally withhold water and keep the rhizome bone dry and warm until fresh growth appears.

For new plants take leaf or stem cuttings, grow from seed, or plant pieces of rhizomes.

To encourage bloom:
Give a definite winter rest.

□ Light shade
□ Temp: 18-21°C (65-70°F)
□ Keep moist and fed

Above: Constant warmth and high humidity will encourage Spathiphyllum 'Mauna Loa' to produce lovely white spathes at any time. The striking flowers, the compact growth and the ability to endure neglect, make this hybrid a desirable houseplant.

 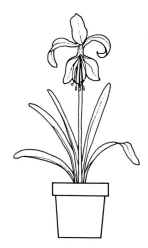

Spathiphyllum 'Mauna Loa'
PEACE LILY
SPATHE FLOWER
WHITE FLAG
WHITE SAILS

Sprekelia formosissima
AZTEC LILY
JACOBEAN LILY

Originally from the Hawaiian Islands, this is truly a very fine plant when grown in conditions that are in tune with its modest demands. The right temperature is one of its most important needs, never less than 18°C (65°F). The roots and the atmosphere surrounding the foliage should be moist, so misting will be beneficial in dry air conditions. Don't overwater though.

In ideal conditions, plants will grow throughout the year and may produce elegant white spathe flowers at any time. Older plants can be divided to produce new ones and these should be potted into a loam-based mixture containing about 50 per cent peat. Place a layer of broken flower pot in the bottom of the container to improve drainage.

Check the undersides of leaves regularly for red spider mites which may infest the plant in too dry conditions.

To encourage bloom:
Keep warm and humid.

□ Light shade
□ Temp: 18-21°C (65-70°F)
□ Keep moist and fed

These are bulbous indoor plants with orchid-like scarlet flowers borne on stems about 50cm (20in) tall in the spring.

The bulbs, which are usually both expensive and in short supply, should be planted with their tips showing in a loam-based mixture that will sustain the plant in the same pot for several years. Following planting, keep in a light and warm place and water freely from the time growth is evident until the foliage dies naturally in the autumn. Then, the soil must remain bone dry until the following year. When flowers appear it will be a signal that feeding with weak liquid fertilizer should begin.

Although frequent potting on is not needed it will benefit the plants to topdress them with new mixture every year. Every four years the bulbs should be repotted and can be divided at the same time to produce new plants.

To encourage bloom:
Observe winter rest period.

□ Sunny location
□ Temp: 10-16°C (50-60°F)
□ Keep moist; dry in winter

Strelitzia reginae
BIRD OF PARADISE FLOWER
CRANE FLOWER
CRANE LILY

This spectacular plant is suitable only where space is adequate; it grows to about 90-120cm (3-4ft) tall when confined to a pot and needs a 30cm (12in) pot when mature. It can be grown from seed but development is painfully slow; from sowing the seed to the production of flowers can be a period of five to ten years. But, if one is patient, the blue and orange flowers are quite a spectacle when they do appear, and have a very long life.

Full sunlight is essential, and plants need potting on when they have filled their existing pots with roots; use loam-based potting mixture at all stages of potting. Feeding is not desperately important and plants will tolerate long periods of draught without appearing to suffer undue harm.

Old clumps can be divided and the sections potted separately. These should flower after two to three years.

To encourage bloom:
Do not disturb mature flowering plants. Grow in sun.

☐ Sunny location
☐ Temp: 13-24°C (55-75°F)
☐ Keep moist; dry in winter

Tillandsia cyanea
PINK QUILL

From a compact rosette of thin green leaves, *T. cyanea* will in time produce one of the most spectacular of flowering bracts, similar in shape to the cuttle fish. The bract emerges from among the leaves and eventually attains a size of about 15 by 7.5cm (6 by 3in). An added bonus is the appearance of brilliant violet-blue flowers along the margin of the bract over a period of several weeks. As one flower dies so another takes its place.

Avoid getting the soil too wet, and never be tempted to pot plants into large containers, as they will be very much happier in smaller pots in free-draining potting mixture. Use a conventional houseplant mix to which chopped pine needles have been added — the latter will keep the mixture open and prevent sodden conditions. Feeding is not important.

To encourage bloom:
Keep warm and humid.

□ Good light
□ Temp: 16-21°C (60-70°F)
□ Water moderately

Left: Strelitzia reginae needs warmth, bright light and space. Its stunning flowers are produced on mature plants during the spring and early summer.

Above: Freesias are elegant, lightly-scented flowers which remain in bloom for many weeks, but high temperatures and airless rooms soon cause the flowers to fade and die.

Index

INDEX